Flights of Faith

Meditations for Flyers

by

Mark Scott

**Magnolia
Mansions
Press**

FIRST EDITION
First Printing, 2000

ISBN 0-9665175-4-7

LCCN: 00-101933

Cover art and design by Carolyn Miller Design

Magnolia Mansions Press
A Division of BOCO Industries
4661 Pinewood Drive
Mobile, Alabama 36618
magnoliamansions@aol.com

To my wife, Karen, who provided the ideas, inspiration, love and support for many happy take-offs and landings.

Taking Off

Every time a plane takes off, passengers and cabin crew are committed to the flight. Think about it. You have no other place to go except your destination. You can't get off the plane. You have made your decision.

Commitment in faith is like that too. When you make a decision to follow God's way to your life's final destination, you should make that decision as if you were riding in a plane gaining speed on a runway.

> *God, grant me the courage to keep*
> *my faith commitments.*

A Whoosh of Fresh Air

Whenever I travel in an airplane, I am bombarded by the air that flows from those little vents above my seat. The air usually comes out just fine, but it is always too hot or too cold. Even if I move the vent so that the air isn't hitting me, I still feel it.

That's what I think God's love is like in my life. I should always feel it, but it shouldn't always make me comfortable. Sometimes God offers me words that are difficult to hear and I am very uncomfortable. Sometimes God offers words of reassurance and hope that come as a gentle breeze blowing over the innermost part of my life.

Lord, blow me away with the power of your Word.

Landings

When you come to the end of a flight, it seems as if you are hovering close to the ground forever. Then, in a sudden "whoosh" you feel the airplane braking, and you look out over the wings to see the inner part of the wing exposed to the rush of oncoming wind. You sit back in your seat and feel the energy of the plane coming to rest on the ground.

In a moment you may be greeting friends or family at the terminal, but for now you have returned safely. You are back on solid ground.

Lord, help me live my entire life on
your solid ground.

Low-Cost Tickets

For the last several years, new airlines have been offering many opportunities for low-cost travel.

When you apply this situation to life, you notice a lot of people who are seeking to find God in the cheapest way too. While low- cost travel may work for many people who fly, the lowest cost is not applicable in life.

God does not ask for partial commitment. God seeks our entire lives and asks that our devotion be complete. And, as Jesus points out, those who seek to save their lives in this world will only end up losing their lives eternally.

*Dear Lord, help me walk the difficult and
costly path as I seek new life in you.*

Fellow Travelers

There are all kinds of stories about people who found each other on airplanes. Often though, people traveling with each other sit alone in silence without caring to know one another as friends.

Traveling with another person does not require commitment. Yet the other passengers I see when I fly remind me that I do not live in isolation. God has blessed me with many gifts of relationship, and some of that blessing may happen when I meet someone new on an airplane.

Thank you Lord for the gift of relationship.

Going Nowhere Fast

One great thing about modern air transportation is the feel of power you gain when you travel far away from home after less than an hour in the air. Every time I fly, I am amazed when I consider where I was only a short time before.

Sometimes life is this way too. Events happen that take us miles from where we have been. In the midst of trauma it is easy to become disoriented or to feel as if we are really going nowhere fast.

If God is really our rock and our salvation in whom we trust, we need not feel this way. God alone will be our help in the midst of trouble.

Dear Lord, help me feel you as my rock.

Overbooking

Sometimes more passengers show up than can fit easily on the airplane. People who give up seats may be rewarded. Others may become disgruntled because they cannot get on that flight.

When you fill your day with too many things, you do the same thing to your life. If too many things dot your calendar, it is also difficult to allow God to flow into your life. Take some time for a "joy stop," and refresh yourself in a renewed feeling of God's grace.

Lord, help me find a retreat from the
busy times of life.

Flying Friendly Skies

Advertising can be a great thing. When one company advertised that we would be flying "friendly skies," the company gave us an image of what living well really means. In life, if you can live as if you were flying "friendly skies," you can discover the real meaning of satisfying relationships.

Just the sound of the phrase evokes a good feeling. Think of your life as a flight. And think of your day as "flying friendly skies."

Lord, help me to be positive and cordial with all whom I encounter in the "friendly skies" of life.

Emergency Exits

You probably don't pay any attention to the emergency exit doors. They just sit there in the airplane, but the people sitting next to them are supposed to be strong enough to help others. When the attendant gives the speech about the doors, no one pays any attention either.

While the speech may not be interesting, it is important. That's the way a lot of other important things are too. We may not want to do some things, but God reminds us that they are still important and we do them anyway. I am really glad for the emergency exits of my life. They help me stay on track.

Lord, keep me focused on the things that are really important even when I seem to lack interest in them.

Encountering Turbulence

You can't see air pockets in the sky, but if you are flying through them, you know they are there. The pilot announces that the plane is passing through "turbulence." Then, he tells you to fasten your seatbelt, and you feel a bouncing sensation in the plane.

Ordinary stuff to a pilot. To passengers who don't travel very much in airplanes, such moments can bring great fears.

Life is that way too. There are times when turbulence comes into our lives. We can't see it coming, but we feel the results anyway. Faith helps us overcome the turbulence and move through it.

Lord, help me overcome the turbulence of my life.

Fasten Your Seatbelt

Those little lighted seatbelt signs above your seat remind you of something very important. When you are taking off or landing, you need to wear a seatbelt. Into the flight, the pilot may take off the light and tell you that you can move around, but the light may also go back on.

Seatbelts offer protection the same way that prayer does. When you wake up in the morning, if you take time to pray, you are really "putting on your seatbelt" for the day.

Lord, give me the discipline to wear
my seatbelt every day.

On Cloud Nine

When you say you are "on cloud nine," you are saying that things are going really well. You are happy. All is right with your life and with the world.

In an airplane you may feel the same way. The puffy, majestic clouds around you can provide a euphoria you feel in no other place. And, in spite of the majesty of you surroundings, it is easy to forget the God who created all of this when you feel you have reached the "top of your game" in life.

On the other hand, it's great to be "on cloud nine" as long as you remember the One who brought you there and take time to give thanks.

*Lord, thank you for all you have provided
in my life.*

In Thin Air

If you tried to ride on a jetliner by attaching yourself to the outside of the plane, you would have a great deal of difficulty. Besides the problem of just hanging on, you would have to breathe in air that contained little oxygen. You would likely become disoriented and eventually you would lose consciousness.

As strange as it may seem, many people live exactly this way. Because of the choices they have made that they may have believed were right, they are living in very thin air morally and spiritually.

God's Word provides good air for everyone to breathe and as you live under God's law you live a full, satisfying life. God's air is not thin. It is rich and pure and fills us with many good things.

Lord, help me breathe in your air.

The People Look Like Ants

An old joke tells about the boy who took his first airplane ride and stated his amazement to the flight attendant that the "people looked like ants."

"I'm afraid they are ants," she replied. "We haven't left the ground."

Every time I fly I remember that joke. As you ascend into the clouds, everything on earth seems smaller, and people appear to be very tiny.

That isn't true with God. With God we are all important and each of us has the potential to receive God's grace as a free gift. As you journey into the clouds, you should find this simple fact very encouraging.

Lord, thank you for making me a special person.

God Is My (Co)Pilot

An old bumper sticker read: "God is my Co-Pilot." Some time after the sticker came out, I saw another that stated "God is My Pilot. I'm only a Passenger."

When we try to bring to ourselves the same power over life that God has, we run into problems. We often make the wrong decisions, and when we seem "God-like" in our decision making, we end up causing pain and heartache.

On the other hand, if God is the Pilot, then we can depend on Him to see us through the crises of our lives and we are freed from worry.

Lord, be my Savior and pilot me.

Beautiful Spacious Skies

Flying over America is great. Thousands of feet below you, life is unfolding for countless people whom you pass at hundreds of miles per hour. It is also unfolding for you as you move from one place to another.

One of the things you notice most about all of this is how vast things seem from the air. Life—the land, the sea, the air— somehow merges into one. In this moment flying becomes an epiphany leading to praise.

Lord, thank you for beautiful and spacious skies.

Peanuts and Cokes

On a recent flight the attendant gave me two one-half ounce packages of peanuts and a Diet Coke. It was part of the "liturgy" of airline travel. At the right moment the attendant asks what you want and brings it to you.

As the flight progresses, the attendant also walks down the aisle of the plane taking up your cup and peanut wrappers.

Maybe peanuts and Cokes are like the wine and bread of airline travel. They are sacred foods of the airline religion.

On a deeper level, peanuts and Coke remind me of the importance of real worship when I am closer to home. They also remind me of the gift of wine and bread as Christ's body and blood. Maybe this is a strange connection. But when you think of it, God's grace is pretty strange to the world too.

Lord, help me see you in many different ways.

Be Careful What You Say

Not long ago, a woman had a headache that just would not go away. When she asked the flight attendant for an aspirin, she told her the headache "hurt so much she could just kill someone."

When the attendant heard that expression, she summoned aid. The plane landed at the nearest airport, and the woman was ejected.

Although not every time that we say the wrong thing will have such terrible consequences, it is really easy to speak in a way that is potentially harmful to others. I doubt that the woman expected to be ejected from the plane, but what she said would have had a dire result if she had acted.

Say what you mean, but remember that meanings can be misconstrued.

God, help me speak the words you
would have me to speak.

On Eagle's Wings

One of the most comforting phrases in the Psalms is the statement that God will bear us up "on eagle's wings." To me this phrase says that no matter what happens in my life, God is there.

Bad things happen. Good things happen. Sometimes nothing happens. Regardless of what happens, God is acting in my life and bearing me up in those moments when I need strength and support.

Like an eagle carrying its fledgling to a new place, so God carries me throughout my life. As you travel, remember the eagle and reflect on the God who is both powerful and comforting in your life.

Dear God, carry me, protect me, and bear me up
on the wings of an eagle.

So What's Playing?

For a long time after I heard about in-flight movies, I never flew on a plane that had one. When I finally boarded a plane with movie screens, I eagerly purchased the headset and began watching.

To my chagrin, not everyone was as entranced by this experience as I was. Most of the people just acted as if they were on a regular flight and the action of the film seemed strangely out of touch with their in-flight routines.

Faith is a little like that too. If you pay attention to God, there will be others around you who could care less about your faithfulness. Don't worry about them. They will never get the plot without hearing the sound.

On the other hand, isn't God calling you to provide the sound?

God, help me to be a better witness.

Stuffing the Overhead Compartment

It is amazing how large some of the luggage is that people bring on board airplanes. Someone will always find a way to place a rather large and bulky suitcase into the rack, and miraculously the door finally encloses it.

Sometimes people try to do the same thing with God that they do with the overhead compartments. They stuff their deeds and actions into a "God compartment" of life hoping that everything will be all right. If you read John 3, you see Nicodemus trying to do this with Jesus.

Fortunately God understands stuffing well. God opens up our lives and offers us a way out—being born again. Jesus said to Nicodemus that he had to be "born of the Spirit," and the same is true for us.

Lord, help me know your Spirit and live as
one born again in you.

21

D.B. Cooper—Child of God

Many years ago a man who went by the name of D.B. Cooper became something of a folk legend after he jumped from a plane in the Pacific Northwest with several hundred thousand dollars of airline ransom money. Cooper was never found, but some of the money was recovered many years later.

If you wonder what happened to Mr. Cooper, the obvious answer is: "Only God knows."

That is however a refreshing thought because the same is true of our lives. Only God knows what will become of you and your life. A knowing God offers a sense of respite and peace in the midst of the chaos of travel. Be calm. Know the Lord and know that the Lord knows you.

Dear Lord, know me that I may serve
as an instrument of your peace.

Mystery and Majesty

As I watch the sky and earth mixed from thirty thousand feet, I always have a certain feeling of mystery. Not only am I traveling faster than my ancestors did, I am traveling in a way that they could only dream about. What was mysterious to them is commonplace to me.

This difference is really one of the failings of our age. Because so many things around us can be explained, we are losing our sense of mystery about life. If we cannot wonder about the gifts God provides, we lose a bit of our faith experience too.

Lord, help me appreciate the mysteries of my life.

Does my Coffee Really Need Whitening?

When my coffee comes, the attendant hands me two sugars and a non-dairy creamer. I haven't asked for it. It just comes with the coffee.

I notice that the package is labeled: "Non-dairy creamer", and I wonder if it really has a purpose. Nothing on the label indicates that milk is remotely related to this product. Yet, if I stir it into my coffee, it will look as if milk has been added, and the coffee will certainly seem creamier.

In life there are many things that pass for something else. Sometimes we ourselves are that way. In order to gain acceptance with a job or a group of people, we become a kind of "non-dairy creamer" to others. We are not "the real thing" and we know it, but if we behave in a certain way, we will be accepted.

It's nice to know that God made me the way I am and accepts me for who I am.

Lord, forgive me when I try to be
someone I am not.

On the Fly

Sometimes this expression refers to eating. Instead of sitting down to eat, we devour a sandwich "on the fly," If you notice people driving and eating at the same time, you realize that this is a very common practice.

The problem is not eating though. When our lives become so hectic that nearly everything we do is "on the fly," then we have a problem.

Quality time for our spirits ought to replace the time we spend "on the fly." If you are reading this while you are flying, you can begin this quality time now. Sit back. Relax. Hear God's voice.

Lord, I pray for your peace.

The Joys of Flying High

When you are "flying high," everything is going right in your life. People assume that you always make the right decisions, and it feels as if everything works in your life.

Unfortunately most of us don't "fly high" often. Our lives plod on from one day to another and we passively take on the tasks that roll into our days.

In spite of this, we can fly high spiritually. God lifts us up to give us the boost we need to fly high in the Spirit. Pause for a moment and imagine yourself flying high spiritually. God promises to raise up all people of faith. God does the work. All we have to do is to fly.

Lord, your grace helps me fly high
whenever I call on you.

Flyin' Real Low

When you are "flyin' low," you may be speeding in a car. Flyin' low also means that you are willing to take risks that you might not otherwise take.

Actually those risks are all around us. We take risks every day that we barely consider. People talk about the risk of the stock market, but they don't think about the pervasive risks of their lives.

Even in our riskiest places in life, the Lord is there. When the risk we take comes out well, the Lord is in our midst. When our risks cause us pain, the Lord is present too.

God, protect me from myself.

27

Eggshells

Sometimes in springtime I notice eggshells on my walking route. The eggshells are a bittersweet reminder of progress.

On the one hand, the shell is a sign that the bird has left the nest. That is a good thing unless you are the bird's mother. As the mother, you would no doubt worry about the safety of the bird you have nurtured in the nest.

On the other hand, the young bird is on its own and learning to fly. It is risking everything that it has on this new venture out in the world.

For the bird, flying is life. Things are not that much different for us either.

Lord, help me meet the challenges
you place before me.

Frequent Flyer Miles

On many airlines, if you fly a certain number of miles in a given time, you are given a free trip as a bonus. I have often wondered about this program.

People who fly regularly are often not at all enthused about the idea of taking still another flight. They want to remain at home, grilling steaks with friends and family. The last thing some of these people want is to cash in those "frequent flyer" miles.

Those people who may not fly very much will find "frequent flyer miles" very enticing and yearn for someone to hand over a few of them.

This dilemma is really a strange image of life. Things that come easily are often valued less. Things that are more difficult to obtain are valued more. With God's grace, the strange irony is that it is free to all who believe and at the same time it is the most valued gift we have.

Lord, help me know your real value in my life.

Flight Time

If you are flying a regularly scheduled airline, one of the things you can depend on is that your pilot has logged many hours of flight time. Essentially this means that your pilot's flying experience minimizes your risk of flying, and there is a certain security in knowing that the people flying the plane know what they are doing.

When Jesus lived among us, he was "logging flight time" too. He was living among people just like us. He was feeling the things that we feel. He was experiencing our problems. And when he went to a cross, he took on everything that the world had to offer.

Lord, thank you for taking on life.

Knowing the Controls

Walking into the cockpit of an airplane is a puzzling experience. There are so many control gauges that you wonder how the pilot can tell them all apart. Thanks to years of training and experience, the pilot is able to operate the plane and guide you safely to your destination.

Although you cannot see them, your life is full of the same kind of control mechanisms that guide an airplane. You focus on the Word of God. You use prayer to guide you and to help you stay on course. You trust that God is capable of bringing you safely home.

God, stay in control of my life.

I'll Fly Away

An old Gospel hymn repeats a familiar refrain, "When I die, Alleluia bye and bye, I'll fly away."

I remember when I first learned this hymn thinking of a bird flying away into the sky. It seemed a fitting image for a return to the arms of the Lord.

With its simple words, the song really states a goal for the spiritual life—to fly away into the arms of a waiting Lord. It is one of those truly soothing images of life.

Lord, help me fly away to you.

Business Class

All the power you need is at your disposal when you fly business class. The airline provides champagne to help you celebrate your conquests abroad. And, if you insist upon working, there is a power supply for your computer next to your seat. Nothing has been forgotten for the modern knights who dash from one continent to another in search of a better life.

Amazingly all the power you need is already at hand, and you really don't need business class flying in order to find it. Spiritual power is yours if you pray for God's guidance and truth.

Lord, restore my power and charge the batteries of my life.

Rosie the Riveter

If you remember the history of the Second World War, you remember the contributions that women made to the war effort by working in the plants that built warplanes.

Many years ago I knew one of the women who worked on those planes. She was one of the most faithful people I have ever known, and she trusted God to provide everything in her life.

I don't really know how many rivets she placed in the planes, but I know she worked at this task with the same dedication and care that she gave to everything else in her life. For her, each rivet would have been important because she knew that riveting was her contribution to victory.

We are like those rivets. God, the great builder uses each of us because God knows how important we are too.

Lord, help me do my part so that
your planes can fly.

Wilbur and Orville

My great-grandfather lived in North Carolina at the time that the Wright brothers were traveling through the state on their way to making their historic flight at Kitty Hawk. According to family legend, one of the brothers happened to meet my great-grandfather.

When my great-grandfather heard of the plans to fly, he responded simply, "She'll never get off the ground."

I'm not sure why we celebrated my great-grandfather's lack of faith and vision so much with this story. Still, his reaction is not much different from the reaction that most people give when they hear about ideas that are strange and different.

Lord, give me the courage to accept new ideas.

Little Travelers

There is something about flying with children that is very enticing. Perhaps because flying is often a new experience for them, there is also a different perspective. Children pay attention to everything. For them the sense of wonder is contagious. Even if the flight is "no big deal" to everyone else, children are filled with a sense of awe.

Perhaps that is why Jesus said that we should be as children. When we experience faith with the eyes of a child, we can wonder about things that we forget to wonder about as adults. The excitement of the faith will be contagious. Not everyone may understand, but it makes no difference. You can be an adult Child of God, but remember the word "adult" must always begin with a small 'a'.

Lord, help me stay excited about my faith.

60,000

At any given moment sixty thousand people in the United States are in the air. Who knows how many are in the air worldwide?

You really don't gain an appreciation of this statistic until you are actually flying at 30,000 feet. Up there, it feels as if there are only a few people in the air, but the statistic reveals a medium sized city flying through the air.

A century ago if you had said that this many people were airborne at the same time, people would have thought you were crazy. All of those planes, filled to capacity and controlled by people watching screens and computers? More importantly all of these people and the ones who watch screens and computers are controlled and cared for... by God.

Lord, help me to appreciate your handiwork.

Waiting on the Runway

There is a lot of waiting at gates in airports. People wait to board planes, and they wait for loved ones to arrive. With all of the traffic created by planes landing and taking off, another kind of waiting is common too—waiting on the runway.

This kind of waiting is even more frustrating than waiting inside a terminal. Your flight has arrived. If only the plane could move a few feet, you can resume your activity. But you are stuck with a couple hundred other hot, angry people inside the plane.

"Call the management," someone suggests. But there is no management to call at this moment. You must wait.

Sometimes life is like that too. You know that God means for you to do something, but the time has not yet arrived. You wait. You may be anxious. You pray. And you wonder when God will give you the resources to perform the task. In the meantime, all you can do is wait.

Lord, give me the patience to be still and listen to you before I act.

Changing Time

If you leave New York flying east toward Europe in the evening, you will arrive in London sometime the next morning. Unfortunately, at your arrival your body will think it is the middle of the night. On your first day in London, your body must adjust to the new time zone, and in the process, you will grow very weary.

Trying to sleep on an airplane in order to beat this situation is a little like sleeping in a hospital room. There are so many distractions. Someone is feeding you; there are movies to watch; your seatmate wants to converse; and you were hoping to finish your novel.

Although the distractions can be annoying, God can and does work through them. Think of the distractions as a gift from God. The food will rejuvenate you. The seatmate needs you to listen because no one else is listening. The movie might help you to pass the time. And, well, you can finish your novel some other time.

Thank you Lord, for the distractions of my life.

Changing Place

You have never been to your destination before. The sights, sounds, and smells of the place intoxicate you with their strangeness. At the same time, being in a new place for the first time can be disorienting.

You don't know exactly how to reach your specific destination. You have to trust a map or the directions of a stranger. You feel vulnerable.

Traveling itself is a faith experience. You have faith that you will return safely and that your luggage will not end up in Cairo when you are in London. Amazingly, most travel crises work out. I prefer not to consider how vulnerable I am when I travel. Yet, I am the same child of God when I travel just as much as when I stay at home. No matter what happens, I have to depend on God's protection and grace.

Lord, help me to see your grace in the
places of my life.

Goin' First Class

One of the most unnerving experiences of flying is sitting in the coach class just behind the first class curtain. You are so close to luxury, but so far, far away. When the curtain is drawn, you begin to fantasize about the extravagant experience of flying first class. What joys are available to the privileged that are denied to the ordinary folks who travel behind them?

Occasionally, the curtain moves. Through the crack you can see people drinking from large wine bottles rather than the miniatures of coach. When you leave, you see that these folks have experienced the flight in seats almost identical to the ones in coach, but with more room between them.

There are all kinds of reasons why people choose to fly first class. Anyone expecting to go first class in the Kingdom of God will certainly be disappointed. As far as God is concerned coach and first class are the same.

Lord, help me overcome my prejudices.

"Barf" Bags

At some point, you knew you would be reading about these things. Many years ago, they were quite obvious in the front of your seat. Now, they are more hidden. Perhaps the airline doesn't want you to think they will be necessary, so they are tucked neatly in some hard to find place so that when you have to use them, they are difficult to find.

Life has its own barf bag. We call it confession. When you confess the things you have done to God or to another person, a load is lifted from your life. It may not be as nasty as the bag on the plane, but it is much more soothing. Confession removes the rough spots from your life and makes you feel whole again. Try it. And, before you go any further, you may want to make sure your bag is in its proper place.

Dear Lord, take my sins on you.

Y2K

Several years ago, no one would have dreamed that this letter-number combination meant anything. As the dawn of a new millennium approached, this was the letter-number combination that spelled potential catastrophe.

Many people were concerned that computers would not be able to read the date "2000" appropriately. And the fear was that on December 31, 1999 a plane might confuse the proper date with the year 1900. Since airplanes were not even invented then, this prospect seemed rather humorous.

What was not humorous were the disruptions that this problem could have caused and the worry that many people felt. What was interesting about this problem was that it was a problem created not by God but by human beings.

Like many things that happen in life, problems come because of human mistakes. There is only one bright aspect to all of the problems we create: God is bigger than our problems are. If you are feeling run down by problems like the worry over Y2K, you should know that God is still in control. Your problems will melt away if you give them to God. And, if you compare the fear some people felt leading up to Y2K to how much they are discussing it today, you realize that some problems really do melt away.

God, give me the faith to turn my problems
over to you.

Bathrooms on Jumbo Jets

On a seven-hour flight, nearly every one of the three hundred passengers on the plane needs to use the restroom. In this situation, only the toughest bladders can make it from one airport to another.

As the flight progresses, a queue begins to form around the toilets at the center of the plane. When your turn finally comes, it feels as if you have entered an airborne port-a-john. In spite of the luxurious seating, the toilet seems sparse and utilitarian. The idea is not to tarry. This is purely a "quick use facility."

In national parks, these "quick use facilities" are sometimes called "comfort stations." Although they are not called that on airplanes, comfort is indeed the purpose that is served. The toilet provides opportunity for better enduring the flight.

When you begin the flight, you may not think there is much value to the airplane toilet. By the fifth hour in the air, it may become indispensable. There are many things like that in life. People or places may not hold much significance to us. However, as we come to know them, they become indispensable parts of our existence and true gifts from God.

Dear Lord, help me appreciate ordinary things.

Flying Animals

When you ride on the inside of an airplane, you really don't give much thought to those who ride in other places. That is, unless you have brought a pet along for the ride.

In order to fly a pet, you must meet the airline's specifications and have the pet properly housed in a crate. I have often wondered what the animals actually think of these things. Do they really enjoy airplane travel or is it just a nuisance to be tolerated?

I suspect that animals are not really fond of the trip. Not only can they not appreciate the experience of flying, they are just another piece of luggage as far as the airline is concerned.

What makes this so difficult is that the people who place them in these containers generally do not believe they are luggage. For them, they are likely to be members of the family.

Flying animals really remind us of how difficult life can be. We care about people we don't always treat as well as we should. Sometimes, treating them poorly is for their own safety. Sometimes, it is for the common good (Not everyone would really want dogs and cats wandering the aisles of airplanes.).

The most important aspect of animals as airline passengers is their safe arrival. Arriving safely is also the most important aspect of our lives too.

Dear Lord, help me to deal with the difficult questions as I journey through life.

First Glimpse of New Land

Flying across an ocean makes you realize just how far apart the continents are. For several hours, you can see nothing but water under the miles of air underneath your plane. Finally, something comes into view that contrasts with the miles of ocean you have passed. Amazingly, no one else seems to notice.

The experience of seeing this land is not nearly so dramatic as it was for the explorers. For you, though, it is a profoundly meaningful experience. You have never been to this country before and seeing the land for the first time is exciting and energizing.

As your plane loses altitude, and the new land comes into full view, you wonder about what it must be like to live here. How has the land shaped the culture? What experiences will await you as you travel to this new place?

I wonder if this experience is a little like what happens when we die. We don't know what to expect. We only know what we know already as the plane lands and we embark on our travel in a new land: God is completely in control and we always live in his care.

Lord, give me the assurance of your love and care.

Whisperjets

Many years ago, Eastern Airlines advertised "Whisperjet service" to the various cities on Eastern routes. If I remember correctly, they even wrote the word, "Whisperjet," on the planes that they flew, and I suppose they wanted you to think their planes were quieter than any others.

Not many airlines give names to their planes. Mostly the manufacturers of the planes are the ones that are mentioned. And, if you fly a Boeing plane, you can tell what you are flying by a three digit number after the name.

I think it would be really interesting if planes had names like American cars. The flight attendant would announce: "Today, you are flying our "Cougar." You would think that you would stealthily arrive at your destination as if you were traveling in a big cat.

Somehow, the airlines have missed a great marketing gimmick. Still, it really makes no difference which plane you fly as long as you arrive safely.

What really makes a difference is that even without a good name for the plane, God knows each of the persons inside that plane and loves and cares for each one of them.

Dear God, thank you for knowing me. Help me know you more completely.

A Window Seat

The best seats on airplanes are always by the windows. However, that sentence is mostly true on shorter flights. When you sit beside a window, you can notice so many things. As the plane sits on the ground before the flight, you notice the activity of other planes around you. As your plane gains momentum on the runway, you notice speed. And, as the plane becomes airborne, you notice the ascent of this leviathan in the sky.

Window seats give you a view of all of this and more. When you have a great window seat, you feel as if you are watching the entire world as you finally gain altitude.

At those times when I imagine what it must feel like to be God, I think of the times I have sat by the window in airplanes.

Yet there are major differences. From 30,000 feet in the air, I can only imagine the lives of the people below me. I cannot know the dreams and aspirations and feelings of these people. I cannot look into their hearts. I can only see the evidences of their lives in the buildings in which they dwell and in the companies where the work.

I find comfort in the differences. God is so much greater than I am, and God knows all of the things I can never even pretend to know.

> *Dear Lord, thank you for taking a*
> *"window seat" over my life.*

A Child Alone

You can see them waiting at the gate. Anxious parents giving last minute instructions to their children traveling alone. "Don't talk to strangers." "Listen to the flight attendant." "Be sure to look for Aunt Mary when you arrive."

If you were to listen closely, you might wonder how the child could remember all of these things. Only the rare ones can.

When I imagine what it must be like to travel alone as a child, I remember the fear and excitement I experienced many years ago when I flew for the first time. I wondered what it would be like. I don't remember much about the flight, but I do remember my fears, and I remember how happy I was to arrive at my destination.

When I think about it, not much has changed. If I am honest with myself, I still feel a lot like that child. New experiences remind me of those old feelings. It is easy to feel like a child traveling alone. The great thing is that with God, we are never alone no matter how desolate and empty life may feel.

Dear Lord, thank you for never leaving me.

Smoking/No Smoking

Before the FAA banned smoking on flights, airplanes felt a lot like bars. If the person next to you was smoking, you had the unhappy lot of breathing smoke for the entire flight. Now, the smell of cigarettes has been replaced by the smell of jetfuel.

With the number of people flying each day, the pervasive odor of too many people in one place consumes the air you must breathe for the duration of any flight.

In a way, cigarette smoke was better. You could at least see it, and you knew that it was there.

All of this reminds me of the inevitable nature of evil. No matter how much we hope to clean up the air in airplanes, something will come along to foul it up. No matter how much we think that we can keep our relationships under control, something comes along to mess them up. No matter how perfect we think we are, something comes along to remind us of our failures and sins.

None of this seems really fair, but that is not the point. Evil works in our lives, and there is nothing we can do to remove it. That is, unless we ask the Lord's forgiveness. Through the power of forgiveness, our lives and our world become clean. No need to ban smoking or anything else. Jesus renews our lives.

Lord, help me deal with the pollution in my life.

Civility

When I was growing up in the 1950's, our family would visit the local airport on Sunday afternoon just to have something to do. Watching the planes take off and land was exciting, and it always seemed so exotic to see people walking off the plane onto those steps they hauled out onto the runway.

In those days, people dressed up to fly. Women wore gloves and hats as they walked down the steps and men wearing suits smiled as they greeted loved ones waiting at the gate. Flying was a cherished and expensive experience.

Today more than forty years later, much has changed. Flying on an airplane is more like riding on a bus used to be. People crowd onto the planes, and sometimes, they don't behave as they should.

Flight attendants are sometimes rude. Passengers sometimes fight with the attendants or with each other. All kinds of things can happen to erase our standards of civil behavior.

I still remember those genteel people who used to fly on airplanes, and I wonder at how much the world has changed. I also wonder if our current experiences in flying might also tell us something about the people we have become. Will we ever discover our gentle spirits again?

Lord, give me patience in uncomfortable situations.

Do Something Religious

Two American pastors, dressed in clerical collars were traveling together with historic communion vessels. They were returning these artifacts to the German congregation that had donated them during the early days when the first settlers had established churches in America.

During the flight, the airplane encountered severe turbulence. Passengers on the plane were beginning to wonder whether or not the plane would arrive safely. When the plane hit an air pocket that forced a sharp lowering of altitude, one of the passengers close to the pastors yelled out: "Quick, do something religious."

Without speaking a word, one of the pastors pulled the ancient communion plate from his briefcase on the floor and began to walk down the aisle. "Okay, I'll take an offering," he piously intoned.

The image of this pastor standing in the aisle broke the tension that everyone was feeling, and a din of laughter began to replace the palpable fear of the situation.

In reality, the pastor did accomplish something religious. He helped people to overcome their fears. That is really the purpose of religion in our lives. Without faith, our fears would cripple us to the point that we could never do anything worthwhile. Faith and laughter go hand in hand to help us to overcome our fears and face difficult moments.

*Lord, give me the faith to laugh even
in moments of peril.*

Air Gourmet

Do you remember when you were little and your mother said that you should eat the food on your plate because there were children in Africa who were starving to death? What she meant to say was that there are people on airlines who would gladly swap the food you were ignoring for the food being served in flight.

Airlines like to pretend that they are offering you food choices. A cheery flight attendant asks: " Would you like the stew or the chicken?" In your mind you imagine dishes that are somewhat different, but when you watch the food being served, it all appears to have the same brown cast.

If the only food served outside the home were served on airplanes, people would live cocooned and isolated in their homes. The entire airline industry would go out of business. Fortunately, food is not the reason most people fly on airplanes.

Amazingly, they eat it anyway. When Jesus fed the multitudes with a few loaves and fishes, I wonder how it tasted. The point was that he could fill their stomachs, but real and lasting spiritual food would be more difficult for them to understand and consume. Airplane food in some ways illustrates that story. Few people would claim that airplane food is the best you can eat yet it serves its purpose: It satisfies your hunger on a long flight.

Isn't that what happens in life too? When we look for ways to satisfy our spiritual cravings and we choose spiritual airline food, we will never be satisfied. However, if we hear the message of the "Bread of Life," we will never be hungry again. Maybe airline food is the way it is so that we will understand the true Bread from Heaven and grow in our faith.

Lord, help me share the true bread
that only you provide.

Before the Flight

"I don't believe in God, but every time I fly, just before the plane takes off, I find myself praying."

When I asked what he was praying about, the things he listed had nothing to do with his own safety. He talked about praying for his wife, and his children, and the people who had been most important to him.

What he was really describing was a long dormant spiritual core somewhere deep inside his being. As life unfolded for my friend, it turned out that he did believe in God. You might say that his spiritual core came to life. He began to read the Bible and even began to go to church regularly.

Maybe when he prayed before a flight, his awakening was just beginning. Maybe God was using the airplane experience to work with him.

My guess is that God does that with us. When you sit down in an airplane there is nowhere else you can go. You have to depend on all of those people and systems that are beyond your control, and even if you don't believe in God, you might pray. After all, God is there for you whether you believe or not.

Lord, use the events of my life to help me believe.

The Beautiful Person in the Next Seat

Nearly every single person fantasizes about the situation. You take your seat beside the window. As you scan the airline magazine, the person you have always wanted to meet takes the seat next to yours.

You wonder what clever line you can say next. Then you think of the breath mint you forgot to take before you took your seat. Then you begin reading your magazine again because you decide the risk of embarrassment just isn't worth it.

The beautiful person sitting next to you remains a mystery. If you take the risk to begin a conversation, your life could change. You could find your soulmate for many happy and romantic flights.

Your conversation could become the key to unlocking an amazing future with this person. On the other hand, if you avoid the risk, you will never know whether or not you have missed an exciting and vibrant relationship.

This situation is a definition for faith. Some people come into new situations and relationships easily. Others require more time.

My advice to you is this: If you are single and you think you might want to talk to the beautiful person seated next to you, don't worry about the breath mint. You only live once and you have no way of guessing what romantic adventure might unfold.

Lord, help me to have courage with faith.

Puddle Jumpers

If you are flying to a small or medium-sized town from a big city airport, there is a good chance you will fly there in a small plane. I don't mean to say that you will feel the air blowing through your hair during the flight. However, after you have hiked to the far end of the concourse, you might wonder just how small the plane really is.

Sometimes these planes are called "puddle jumpers." I suppose the idea is that because they are small, they can land between puddles. Unfortunately, because they are small, you might not have as much confidence in them as you would have in larger planes.

Maybe a flight on a "puddle jumper" is not as big an act of faith as you think it is. However, when you notice that there are only three other passengers on the flight, and a summer thunderstorm is lurking in the weather forecast, you really might wonder if you have chosen the wrong way to get to Peoria.

Many larger airlines use these smaller carriers as subsidiary companies they call "commuter airlines." Generally all the word "commuter" means in the title is that the planes are small and there is no way you will be comfortable once you are in your seat.

I think commuter planes are really an image of our special individuality. God didn't create us to be superjets capable only of long distance travel. God meant for us to jump through the puddles of life and visit those rare and unique places that appear as tiny dots on the map. God even meant for some of us to live in those places. And God meant for each of us to live as his own special people.

When you think about it, if you flew to visit the greatest or most holy people in history, you would need a "puddle jumper." After all, if the New Testament were set in today's world, the wise men could never have flown a jumbo jet to Jerusalem International Airport. They would have had to fly in a "puddle jumper" and rent a car for the drive to Bethlehem.

Lord, help me remember the
"specialness" of my life.

Air Babies

I have never understood how people are able to fly with babies. Often, without a seat for themselves, they must endure the trip in the arms of a parent.

While traveling on airplanes with babies, there is only one rule: The longer the flight, the more difficult it will be to keep the baby happy. The corollary to this rule is that the larger the number of small children on a flight, the more difficult it will be to keep all of the rest of the passengers happy.

This is particularly true if there is a drop in cabin pressure during the flight. Wails overtake the silence, and fear overcomes the calming effects of the perpetual noise of the airplane engines.

If you are a passenger traveling without a baby in tow, it may be difficult to appreciate the children on your aircraft if this situation develops. As you listen to incessant crying, you might come to realize that children are a real barometer of flight comfort. If the trip is short and uneventful, small children remain calm. On the other hand, if there is some difficulty, the organization in the cabin disintegrates.

In life, children can be gauges for many situations and events. If you pay attention to children, you may also discover important things about their parents.

This must have been what Jesus meant when he invited little children to come closer to him claiming that they represented the Kingdom of God. With that thought in mind, it is probably best that Jesus never flew in an airplane with two dozen babies at feeding time.

Lord, help me appreciate the gift of children even when I cannot appreciate their behavior.

Turbulence at Night

Until you fly at night, words such as "updraft" or "downdraft" are just meaningless weather words. In the stillness of the evening on a flight across the Atlantic when the only light in the airplane is coming from the television screen in front of you and you are drifting off to sleep, a downdraft can be a terrible reality.

Suddenly, your world becomes very small and you wonder not only about the skill of your pilot but whether or not the engineer who designed the plane really knew what he was doing the day he determined how much turbulence your aircraft could endure. As the hulking monster of a plane ratchets back and forth in the darkness, you awaken and focus your attention on the movie hoping that calmer air will soon prevail... It doesn't.

As the turbulence continues, silent darkness churns within your stomach. If you are philosophical, you may wonder if God really is a hole in your being aching to be filled. No matter what you think, you are just a passenger in the night hoping that the turbulence will soon end.

There are many times in life when it feels as if nighttime turbulence will never cease. As time passes and Europe draws closer, you notice that the sun begins to drench the darkness in an eerie morning glow. Darkness gives way to color as the land beckons in the east. The engineer was right. Your aircraft can endure the turbulence.

As the knowing engineer of the universe, God enables each of us to endure the turbulence we face in life. Downdrafts and updrafts come into our lives, and like the aircraft, we do endure. Try to forget the turbulence and sleep. God will take care of you.

> *God, help me pass through the turbulence*
> *to life's good times.*

Computerized Flying

"Just wanted to inform you," the pilot's voice seemed friendly as it chirped through the speakers on the plane as we taxied toward the terminal, "that the landing you have just experienced was completely managed by our on-board computer."

"According to FAA requirements," he continued. "We have to test this computerized landing system at least once a month and today was the day we tested it."

"Of course, had there been any real problems, we would have executed a runaround and made the approach again."

As the pilot delivered this news, there were audible groans in the passenger cabin. This was news most of the passengers could have gone all day without hearing. Still, for some reason, the captain thought that knowing this information would make all of us feel a little better about our computer driven landing.

Sometimes God encourages you this way too. In times of questioning, it is easy to ignore the spiritual purpose God has for your life and to know as the pilot did that God can always execute a "runaround." It is also easy at such times to tune God out or to listen to different messages than the ones God would have you hear.

Like the pilot announcing the happy message of a successful landing, God helps you understand that things will be all right. Your journey will conclude safely and successfully. After all, God is always with you.

Thank you God for being at the controls of my life.

MEDITATIONS
FOR THE
CONCOURSE

Time Flies

Long before the age of flight, people started using the phrase "time flies.". The idea of course is that there is never enough time in the day to do the things we need to do.

You may not believe this however, if you are waiting for a plane to take off three hours from now. This kind of time does anything but fly. The minutes inch painfully along. You may wonder what you will do with all of that time.

Remember that even time that you cannot easily fill is a gift from God. Try to use the gift in a way that is satisfying to you and to God.

God, help me use the gift of time to the fullest.

Killing Time

I wonder if "killing time" is covered in the Ten Commandments. If it is a violation of the commandment to kill, then killing time must be a violation too.

Killing time is a strange thing though. Sometimes it is easier than we think. Time just oozes from our lives and we sometimes have no control over it. And, of course, at other times, we wish we could find something to pass our time better.

Ancient monks ordered their time around the hours of the day, and they worshiped knowing that praising God was not killing time at all. When you kill time, you are really killing a resource that God has entrusted to you. Maybe now is a good time to use this moment to pray for forgiveness.

Lord, forgive me for killing time.

No Laughing Matter

The first thing I see as I walk up to my gate is a sign stating that security is no joking matter. "Everything that you say will be taken seriously."

I'm really glad I don't have to live at this gate, but I know the reason for the sign. If everything anyone said were always totally serious, then life would be pretty depressing.

In the concourse, nearly any joke will do, but don't say anything about luggage or airplanes.

Thank you God for humor.

Ducks in a Row

Nearly all of the airports I have seen have the same problem with concourse seating. There is no way for people to converse with each other easily. I can just imagine some airport architect concluding that most people will be traveling alone, so there would be no need for people to speak with each other.

Airport waiting areas look as if they were designed for ducks. Everyone sits neatly in rows. Sure the rows aren't very long, but is this what life is about?

I don't really expect a waiting area to reflect community experience, but I am also thankful that I have opportunities to be around other people in more intimate surroundings. Everything has its purpose. The waiting area of the concourse hopefully is not your life.

Dear God, thank you for the people
who are close to me.

Shut Up and Mind Your Own Business

It was early in the morning. A single mother was traveling with her daughter and son, and the little girl did not want her mother to comb her hair. Her brother made a smart remark. The little girl who could not have been more than five shouted loudly: "Shut up and mind your own business."

No one seemed to pay any attention, and to the girl's dismay, her mother continued to comb her hair.

The concourse is a picture of everyday life. Families annoy each other. People come and go. Reunions occur. Refugees arrive. For the most part, we do mind our own business, but we are all connected by God's abundant and overwhelming love.

Dear Lord, thank you for caring for me and not just minding your own business.

Dealing Drugs

I once had a neighbor whose job was to stand around in the Atlanta airport looking for drug dealers. He was interviewed for an article in the paper about this odd and interesting line of work.

He told the reporter that there was a good chance you could spot drug dealers because of they way they dressed, and that all he really did was to look for a certain type of person coming into the concourse.

If it's that easy to read shady characters, think about how God can read your life. Also consider that even though God knows you, God still forgives you if you have a repentant heart. Amazing isn't it?

Dear God, Help me trust your amazing grace.

Check Out the Plumbing

Some of my favorite public restroom facilities are in large new airports. They never have doors, and you can carry your luggage right in. Also, the toilets flush automatically, and they have those wonderful sinks which only require that you place your hand under the faucet. It feels as if someone is there helping you, but you can't see the person helping at all.

For me that kind of restroom is a little like my image of God. I can't see God, but when I need something to cleanse my soul, I can pray and I know God is there.

Lord, thank you for your visible and invisible love.

The Baggage Inside

One of the first things you notice as you move through the concourse is a machine that inspects your baggage. Beyond the metal detector, someone looks through the eye of a machine at all of your personal belongings.

This small invasion of privacy in the name of security gives strangers a godlike quality. They don't know you, but they know what you are carrying. And, if you are holding the wrong things, you will be detained.

How different this is from the way God looks into the baggage of our lives! God sees all of our baggage and could easily cast us away. Instead, God accepts us with redeeming and forgiving love. Could we ask for more than this?

Dear Lord, thank you for accepting me even with the baggage I carry.

Keep Away from the Door

The train in the Atlanta airport has a message for you if you tarry too long at the door as you are entering. "Keep away from the door" the message blares as people glare in your direction. You have violated a rule and the doors are very unforgiving. No one can move until you move. For an instant the whole system depends on you.

Jesus said that God loves the birds of the air so we don't have to worry about our own lives. When you suffer the insults of computer-generated voices, Jesus' words are good to remember. God blesses us even if we are embarrassed by the lack of blessing from others.

Dear Lord, thank you for forgiving
me when I make mistakes.

Rotating Baggage

One of the most intriguing things about the airport is the baggage claim area. When you arrive at your destination, you have the tedious task of watching luggage rotate until yours comes into view. Sometimes this becomes quite a show as people drag all of the things they have gathered from the baggage cafeteria.

I have sometimes wondered if heaven might be like the baggage area. When your journey on earth is complete, you remain on some mythical conveyer until the time is right. Then, like some piece of baggage, St. Peter pulls you from the rotation, and you enter heavenly splendor.

Fortunately the comparison really doesn't work. Life and luggage are not the same thing. The Bible promises that God will receive all who believe (Romans 3:25-28), so baggage claim really has little to do with heaven anyway.

Jesus, remember me when you
come into your Kingdom.

Checking In

Ticketless travel is really interesting. In order to board your flight, you simply show a photo ID, and they give you a boarding pass. As you wait to board the plane, the pass becomes your ticket.

I wonder how much this process resembles entry into heaven. Somebody hands out passes to those waiting to enter. Beyond the door is a corridor that leads not to a plane but to the riches of eternal life.

Lord, remember my boarding pass when I come into your Kingdom.

Flight Questions

"Has this luggage been in your possession for the last twenty-four hours?" "Did anyone hand you anything to bring onto the flight?"

Standard questions. Security. I wonder why they insist on asking these questions. Who would answer affirmatively?

All kinds of questions pry information from us in this life. I am really glad that God already knows the answers.

Lord, give me the patience to deal with questions.

Laying Over

When the weather is really bad, local television cameras record the painful circumstances of those who must wait in airports. Interviews reveal the obvious fact that time passes very slowly.

Drawn and fatigued faces report the anxious moments of waiting and the longing to return to friends and family.

Finally the planes fly again and not a moment too soon. The waiting completed, the journey begins. Life in microcosm.

Lord, help me endure the wait.

Local Color

Not long ago, an article described the different foods you could purchase in different baseball parks. What the article seemed to say was that menus made the parks special.

I often wonder about what you can tell about places if the only place you go is the airport. You really have to look to glimpse any image of local color, and unless you pay special attention, all airports seem the same.

Saying that all airports are alike is almost like saying that all people are alike. In a way, it is true. In another way, it is totally false.

Lord, thank you for all the unique places
inside my life.

The Roar of the Engines;
The Smell of the Jetfuel

The airport concourse is shaped not only by a sense of space but also by the sounds and smells that permeate the environment. Underneath the soft music that bombards your senses is the hum of planes going back and forth to runways and the smell of the jetfuel that propels them.

This makes the airport an image of creation. But it is a creation entirely made by human hands.

Compare this to the majesty of God's creation, and you begin to sense the majesty and mystery of God. Human beings can do many things. Only God can create.

How great and majestic is your name, Oh God!

Skycaps

An article I read about skycaps revealed that some of them make a lot of money helping people with baggage in the airport terminals. I was surprised by the article only because I had never considered the situation before.

Then I realized that the skycaps are rewarded with money for something that many people do without thinking. They serve. People express gratitude for those who serve well, and sometimes money is exchanged.

Think about ways you serve because of your spiritual motivations. Serving without need for reward is one of life's greatest blessings.

Lord, help me serve graciously.

The Moving Sidewalk

Moving sidewalks are really wonderful. You can walk twice as fast because the sidewalk under your feet is moving too. Even if you are walking slowly, you move quickly.

I often feel as if the years of my life are being lived on a moving sidewalk. Looking back, I wonder about how quickly the time has passed. What has happened to my life? Why haven't I done the things I thought I should have done at twenty-five? What else can I do in my business? How much of a future can I really have?

Perhaps you have the same or similar questions about your life. As I reflect on how quickly time passes, I also realize that speed is only a perception. God gives each of us a certain number of days that we count as a gift of time. If we make use of that time as a gift, then it makes no difference whether it passes quickly or slowly.

What is important to God is that we use the gift wisely as we spend time with others. The questions we should ask should relate to whether or not we have treated others fairly. Have we loved others and ourselves? Have we adequately served others in business dealings? Have we treated others fairly?

In other words, God is concerned about questions of relationship rather than questions of time.

Lord, help me use the time you have allotted to me.

A Stairway to Heaven

Airports do not have the longest escalators I have ever seen, but they come close. It always feels as if people are moving on a giant stairway to heaven, and the escalator is the conveyance.

If there were some kind of "stairway to heaven," I believe it would be a lot like an airport escalator. All kinds of different people would be on board, and they would have come to the escalator from many different perspectives of understanding. But once they hopped on the escalator, they would all be going to the same place. The point is that God accepts each of us as we are. We just have to enjoy the ride.

Lord, help me onto your "stairway to heaven."

Air Art

Art in the terminal is interesting. Some people may even understand it. Mostly though, the art is design art that is supposed to add color to the otherwise austere and cavernous walls of the terminal.

Don't misunderstand me. I think that "air art" is good. But I wonder how it all came to be. Did some committee decide that it ought to be in a certain location? Or was there some "terminal creator" who on the seventh day decreed: "Let there be art."? Or, did some design consultant decide that a particular piece of art would "speak volumes to the traveling public."?

I think that we ought to take "air art" on spiritual terms. Like creation itself, it is there to be enjoyed. Understanding it is secondary to appreciating its presence. There are many things we do not have to understand in order to appreciate. Think of "air art" as one of them.

Lord, help me give thanks for all works of creation.

Passing through Customs

One of the onerous experiences of travel is having to go through customs as you arrive home from a foreign visit. On the plane, they hand you a slip of paper which gives you the "opportunity" to declare all the purchases you have made since you have been away.

Unless you are a C.P.A., this figure will likely turn out to be wrong. Then, you sit there wondering, "What if they say I brought in more than I say I did? How much will I really owe in customs duties?"

For the rest of your flight the form you filled out causes you to worry. Usually (but not always), the customs agent looks knowingly into your eye and determines that what you have stated is reasonably true. Relieved, you pass through the turnstile. You are home again.

I can't help wondering if this isn't a little like the experience of dying. Like some slip of paper you have filled out, your life flashes before God, and you wonder if what you have stated through your words and deeds will really be good enough.

With infinite grace, God waves you through the turnstile to a new life full of possibility and excitement. And there, as you pass through the turnstile in bold letters are the words: REJOICE AND GIVE THANKS! YOU ARE HOME!

God, when my time comes, receive me
with your infinite grace.

Making Sense of the Confusion

When you walk through the automatic doors of any major airport, you are likely to encounter a confusing array of logos for airlines. Airlines are like religious groups or denominations. They all think they have something unique, and they mostly want to convince you that they are the best means to bring you to your destination.

Making sense of the confusion in the airport means that you trek to the counter of the airline that is serving you. In a way, the airport is like the world. Making sense of life means that you trek toward the message that provides you with meaning. Life can be just as confusing as that first feeling you get at the airport.

Thankfully, God responds in the midst of the confusion to show the way to Truth.

Lord, lead me to your Truth.

On or Off

"I figure that flying is like a trip to the dentist's office." My friend announced. After my puzzled response, she explained what she meant. "I mean, if you make the appointment with the dentist to have a tooth pulled, you know you will pay him something no matter what. Until you actually sit in the chair and go under the anesthetic, you can always walk away."

I had never thought of it that way before. However, as I thought of what she said, it made sense. Life is really a lot like that. Some experiences in life we crave more than others. Some people want to fly whenever they get the chance. Others regard it as a trip to the dentist's office. And, the amazing thing is that no matter how we view such things, we view them from our own individual, God-given perspective. That, in itself, is reason to give thanks.

Dear Lord, thank you for my point of view.

Finding Your Place

If you drive to an airport, you may find that long term parking leaves you with quite a hike. Cars are all over the place. After a while, all of them begin to look so much alike that you begin to wonder how you will ever find your car when you return from your trip.

The words of the "Cheers song" from the old television show begin to come to you: "Making your way in the world alone takes everything you've got." You wonder how you will catch the flight you have scheduled in just twenty minutes.

A place comes into view. You park and forget the tension of the last five minutes. As you settle into your airplane seat, the chaos of airport parking is a world away. You have found your place and what a good feeling it is.

Perhaps this situation is a very small mirror of things that are happening in your life. You want to make a difference, but you can't quite figure it out. Are you driving aimlessly in an infinite parking lot? Is no place yet in view?

If that is the case, remember that you will eventually find your way. There is purpose for your life. God created you to be special and unique and to make your special and unique contributions.

Lord, help me keep finding the place
where I can contribute.

On-Time Performance

This is the one phrase related to airline travel that provides the greatest problem. Airlines struggle to make schedules. Irate passengers wonder why airlines cannot place them on time to their destinations. And thousands of people must take later flights because of overbooking.

On-time performance is a difficult concept when the planes are full. Yet all of the airlines compete for the claim of the having the most "on-time" flights.

This competition reminds me of how difficult it is to achieve perfection. No matter how hard the airlines try, none will ever find that all flights are "on time." It just won't happen.

Fortunately God is not an airline. God knows our frailties, shortcomings, and weaknesses. God will never judge us the way that J.D. Power and Associates judges airlines. In spite of all of our failures, God receives us into the Kingdom and blesses us with abundant and overwhelming love. It's a gift we call "Amazing Grace."

Dear Lord, help me hear your
word of amazing grace.

Folded, Spindled, and Mutilated

Sometimes things don't turn out too well in airports. Luggage is damaged or lost. Valuables are misplaced or broken. Flying itself can leave a traveler feeling as if he or she were a piece of worn out luggage dragged along some conveyer belt. Modern airline travel can leave nearly anyone feeling folded, spindled, and mutilated.

If you are feeling that way as you read this, take a moment to revive your spirit. Close your eyes. Take a deep breath. Try to separate yourself from the stress of the moment. Pray a prayer asking God to give you the serenity that will give you a stronger sense of wholeness.

Life should be a joyful experience. Feeling folded, spindled, and mutilated is NOT the way that God means for you to live. God can bear your burdens, but you must give them over to God.

Dear God, help me place my
burdens in your hands.

Making Connections

Anyone who has ever flown very much knows this dilemma: You have a plane to catch ten minutes after you land. The problem is that you have to be at the other end of the airport.

Frantically you move from one concourse to another wondering if the plane will take off without you. Relieved, you finally arrive at the gate to learn that the flight you are boarding has been delayed by twenty minutes.

At this point you don't know quite what to feel. Should you feel gratified at your success? Or should you feel angry because of the delay?

Relax. Twenty minutes is not that long compared to your whole life. This is God's gift of time.

Dear Lord, give me patience with the
things beyond my control.

Tickets on the Internet

A growing number of airline tickets are being sold electronically over the Internet. A computer screen, a few keystrokes, and there it is—your confirmed reservation. No need for human contact for something so mundane as an airline ticket! This is real progress!

To be sure it is far more convenient to purchase your ticket this way. Yet this is also one more example of our lack of need for others. Internet ticketing also reminds me of something that has been lost.

Advancing technology often causes us to lose our connections with each other. Like cities of lonely people, airports collect those on their way to all kinds of places. They carry baggage you can see and baggage that cannot be seen—the stories of heartbreak and joy in people's lives. Everyone you see in this imaginary city needs to be loved.

Look around you. Think of the lives the strangers beside you are living. Think of their need to be loved. And say a prayer of thanks for the God who loves us all!

*Dear Lord, help me appreciate everyone
around me.*

Chapel at Gatwick

While I was standing in a queue at Gatwick Airport, a crisp English voice announced, "There will be a chapel service for all who wish to attend at 10:30 a.m."

"Too bad," I thought. "My plane leaves at 11:00."

For the rest of the morning, though, I wondered about that service. What would it be like? Who would be there? What sort of worship would include any interested person at Gatwick Airport?

Finally I realized that the few were praying for the many. I felt a sudden comfort knowing that someone was taking the time to pray for my safety and the safety of everyone else who traveled that day. This prayer I would never hear became an invisible safety net for my journey. And as I considered the gift of this service, I prayed that those still worshiping as my plane taxied down the runway would be inspired as God was glorified. It felt good.

Lord, help me use your gift of prayer.

Concourse Shopping

Shopping in airports is both interesting and unnerving. If you had to live on the things you can purchase in airports, you would be wearing T-shirts and eating junk food. People would know you had been somewhere, but if you never left the airport, they would think you led a very boring life.

In other words, shopping in the concourse is more than a little incomplete. It meets some needs but not others.

Longing for completeness or wholeness is a basic issue in human life. Most of us would not choose to spend our lives in airport concourses. They are simply stopping points on the way to somewhere else.

Sometimes life is like our airport shopping experiences. Things feel incomplete. The things we do or the people with whom we have relationships do not really meet our needs. We have big holes in our lives that need to be filled.

No shopping mall in the world could compare with the completeness that God brings to our lives. With prayer and faith and our openness to God, then the holes begin to be filled. We come to new understandings. And, best of all, our spiritual wardrobe expands. We don't have to go around all the time dressed in T-shirts.

Lord, help me become complete and whole.

Your Secret Lounge

Some airports, have special places reserved for frequent flyers. These places are removed from the thousands of other travelers in the airport and are supposed to provide a tranquil time away from the hustle and bustle of people rushing from one flight to another.

I have never been in one of these places and for me, they are mysterious and surreal. I imagine a place of soft music and dim lights in which the weary traveler might be immersed in tranquility. Large aquariums containing oversized goldfish floating aimlessly in their tanks provide a visual getaway that makes you forget why you are in the airport.

I really don't want to go into one of these places because the reality would upset the mystery. I would realize that they are simply nice places where people stop but do not stay.

There is a secret lounge for each of us. It is called prayer. When we take time to pray, we have the opportunity to get away from the routines of our lives. We access the mystery of God. And we discover a tranquil place inside us that we may not have known.

Shut your eyes. Try to relax. You are moving into your secret lounge.

God, help me find the words to pray.

Red-Eye Special

Late at night airports are pretty lonely places. Cleaning crews clean up the flotsam of the day. A few forlorn agents stand behind airline counters like weary survivors of battle. Travelers appear from time to time making their way to flights that leave at times when most people are in bed.

In this setting the airport becomes a cauldron for human loneliness. If you look around, you might wonder if anyone ever cares for anyone else. Everything seems disconnected. And if you think about it too long, you might become really depressed.

Perhaps you are reading these words in such a setting. As you pay attention to this kind of loneliness it is easy to wonder if God cares when no one else seems to care. When the psalmist wrote: "Out of the depths I cry to you O Lord..." he could not possibly have been thinking of lonely evenings in airports.

Yet such times are modern expressions of the depths everyone faces in life. The Psalmist knew something that all people of faith know: The Lord is there even in the depths. The Lord hears our prayers. We are not alone. Stay focused on that knowledge even when loneliness seems to crowd out the other, more vital parts of your life.

Lord, listen to the prayers of my lonely heart.

Check Your Baggage

After waiting the ten minutes that feel like an hour, you finally come to the front of the line. An agent who is paid to smile greets you pleasantly and asks where you will be flying today.

Without thinking you place your bag on a large piece of metal, and a digital readout tells you how much it weighs. The agent quickly slips a piece of paper onto your luggage and moves it onto a conveyer belt.

Congratulations! You have just made a statement of faith. You have entrusted the airline with your precious baggage in the hope that it will arrive safely with you at your destination.

If you read the consumer reports on airlines, you know that your faith in the safe arrival of your baggage is not a foregone conclusion. Different airlines have different rates of delivery, and rooms are set aside in airports for people looking for lost luggage.

While you can pinpoint the placing of your baggage on the airport scales as an act of trust, you make all kinds of faith statements every day of your life. Most of these statements do not even cross your mind. Taken together, your actions tell people a lot about the things you believe in.

I wonder what the counter agent would think if everyone placing bags on the scales stated with conviction: "I am acting on my faith. I believe that this bag will arrive with me at my destination!"

Lord, help my actions speak
as loudly as my words.

The Queue

It sounds so English: "The Queue." In America, they just describe it: "The long wait," "The line," "It went on forever." "I thought I would never get out of there." "The line was so long that my youngest child was out of college before I could get to the checkout counter."

With the traffic in airports, it is a minor miracle that people really do reach their planes after they have checked their baggage. You would think that the agent was taking an inventory of people's lives instead of simply placing their baggage on an airplane.

What amazes me about "the queue" is how patiently people endure the time spent waiting. I know that Americans are less equipped for this kind of wait than people in other countries. I know that there are horror stories of irate passengers who could not take it anymore. For the most part though, people manage these situations.

I think we manage them because they are so much like the rest of our lives. If you think about your day, there are few moments when things are really exciting. Most time is mundane, and much of it is waiting time.

To me, this is an opportunity for peace rather than tension. Use your waiting time as prayer time. Memorize a prayer you can say over and over again. Feel the rush of tranquility in the midst of chaos.

> *Dear Lord, help me not to waste*
> *the queues of my life.*

Lost Luggage

I once visited a store in Boaz, Alabama, that sold the luggage that people had lost in airports. There was so much of this luggage displayed that the store had the musty odor of old suitcases. Neatly hung rows of belts and ties were evident throughout the store. And there were also more interesting items for sale such as skis, golf clubs, and tennis rackets.

For me what made the store so interesting was the variety of things that were lost. I looked at some items and wondered why anyone would try to take them onto an airplane. But there they were. Amazingly these items were not lost forever.

As I walked out of this store, I thought about how much it must be like heaven. That which is lost is found. That which was worthless now has value once again.

In a way that is how God views our lives. We are a lot like that lost luggage. We could stay lost. But remarkably someone finds us, restores us to goodness, and pays a price for us. However, this is where the analogy fails. In the end God makes us new and gives us new life. I don't think anyone would really want to end up in a store for lost luggage.

Dear Lord, your "Amazing Grace" really is a sweet sound. Thank you for finding and claiming my life.

Getting to the Airport

It's the day before Thanksgiving, and you are flying home for the holiday. You only have a few days of vacation time, and you have looked forward to your trip since last September when you made your reservations.

Pulling out of your driveway, you instinctively turn up your radio only to hear a traffic report: "All interstate highways leading to the airport have very heavy traffic. Allow an extra thirty minutes for your trip."

"No problem," you say to yourself. "I've got plenty of time."

At the same time you make this brave statement, you worry whether or not you will be able to negotiate the traffic in town just to get to the airport.

Anyone who has ever traveled on a holiday weekend knows this experience. Local TV stations have a standard feature they run at this time of year interviewing people who expect to take flights during peak hours. They also seem to air an interminable series of reports about how awful the traffic is on the highways leading to the airport.

I suspect that most people would rather do without these "news features." We have enough to worry about without thinking of the heavy traffic in airports. Give me a short statement about traffic conditions on the highways, and I will figure out an alternate route.

Unfortunately though, life does not work that way. There are countless times in life when you get bogged down before you get started. Clogged highways are just one picture of many that take place under other circumstances in our lives.

Naturally things don't have to turn out badly. You will make it to the airport. Your plane will fly. You will be safely home for Thanksgiving. And you will return home safely.

Between now and then, there will be a few challenges along the way. Take a moment to pray for patience. You will overcome them.

Lord, help me overcome the challenges
and obstacles I face each day.

Duty-Free Shop

In larger airports, one of the shops you sometimes see is the "Duty-Free Shop." The allure of this shop is also quite interesting. Things that carry large duties are sold at incredibly cheap prices.

Ironically, while you may be able to purchase these items cheaply, most of the things the store sells are not very good for you. Cigarettes cause cancer. Liquor can be addictive. The fat in chocolate will clog your arteries.

If you took these items out of the duty-free shop, they really would not have too many other things to sell. So the real message of the duty-free shop is: Avoid the duty now, but remember you will pay later.

When you think of it, there are all kinds of duty-free shops around that entice you into one behavior or action. Only later do you realize that the enticement has not been in your best interest.

The Bible has a word for avoiding bad behavior. The word is "righteousness." Righteousness may not give you an immediate feeling of pleasure, but when you act righteously, you gain the satisfaction of knowing that you have done the right thing. You are a person of real character. And ultimately you will live with real and genuine joy.

In the meantime, purchase what you want at the duty-free shop. Just know that much of what you buy will carry some kind of "duty" anyway.

Lord, help me lead a righteous life.

Baggage on Wheels

You don't have to sit around the waiting area of the concourse very long before you see someone rolling a suitcase on wheels.

This simple innovation shows just how far the baggage industry has come over the last century. Years ago when people traveled it seemed that they took all of their possessions with them. Large trunks stored clothes that could not be packed in any other container.

Then for years people carried suitcases with handles. Now they carry their baggage so easily that you wonder if they are aware they have it.

I once saw a man who carried a cross around with wheels. An article in the paper noted that the man saw this as his personal ministry. He was carrying a cross to remind people of the price that Jesus paid for their lives.

Whenever I see someone rolling a suitcase on wheels, I think of that man I saw on the highway. No matter how many innovations we make, we can never really get rid of our baggage. It follows us wherever we go.

The problem of course, is that most of the baggage we carry won't fit into a suitcase. We use difficult words to describe that baggage: guilt, shame, hatred, remorse, anger.

You don't really have to go anywhere to carry that kind of baggage, but if you have it, it follows you wherever you go.

And it can be as heavy as an old steamer trunk. Think about your baggage. And pray to God to take it from your life.

Lord, remove from my life the baggage
I don't really need to carry.

Seating Configurations

It's thirty minutes until they call your flight, and the only thing on your agenda is to sit and wait until it's time to board.

You look around. Other people are fewer than ten feet away, but the seats are not made for conversation, they are made for waiting. Maybe they were designed so that as many people as possible could sit in this space, but the arrangement does not seem very friendly. You sit and wait—alone.

As you stare into space, a little girl comes along and breaks your inner silence. "Where are you going?" She asks. Then, before you can answer, she blurts out, "I'm flying with my grandmother to summer camp."

Intrigued by her overt friendliness, you look up and notice the grandmother offering a scolding look to the little girl for her violation of your space. You smile. "It's all right. I needed someone to talk to."

No longer are the seats just places where people wait. Life is shared. Small friendships form.

There is something about traveling that demands companionship. Maybe that's what we mean when we say we are human.

Lord, help me appreciate my companions in the pilgrimage of life.

Hearing Voices

Airports are full of voices. Most of them are mysterious and unexplainable. "Mr. Owen Benson please come to gate A 23. Your party is waiting to meet you there."

Even though you don't know Mr. Benson or his party, you listen. Why hasn't he shown up? Maybe he really didn't want to get married. Maybe he is just late. Maybe he's taken a different plane.

Cellular phones still do not solve all of these minor communications problems. People forget to call. Genuine excuses do occur. And the voices intone the results of our failures: "Your party is waiting. Where are you?"

Hearing voices can also be a positive part of life. God speaks. We listen. We act on our listening: Go. Serve. Live in faith.

Sometimes the voice seems so direct. Sometimes it seems so indefinable. Can you hear the voice directing your life?

Dear Lord, help me listen when I hear your voice.

Remote Locations

If you live in a place that is not served by many airlines, you may face a painful reality: Flying is always expensive. Well, maybe not always. You could be one of the four or five lucky passengers on the flight holding a discounted ticket.

For the most part though, you could save a lot of money driving three or four hours to a major city in order to take advantage of the cheaper travel opportunities there. In the game of discounted airline fares, it is easy to feel that you have been left out because you live in the wrong place.

Feeling left out is a common problem in life. People struggle to find groups or clubs to which they can belong. Sometimes they never succeed. The yearning to belong leads some into struggles with alcohol or drugs. Or this struggle simply leaves others with a nagging and relentless loneliness that never seems to go away.

Belonging is an essential part of what God has in mind for you. With God there is never a question of whether or not you will be good enough to belong or whether you live in the right city or have the "right address." God receives everyone who believes into his Kingdom. All we have to do is to know that we belong... to God.

Dear God, help me feel that I belong to you.

Arrivals and Departures

When you walk into an airport, one of the first things you look for is a board listing the arrivals and departures for the day. Flight numbers, words, and places flow together to create a strange art form: Flight 8726 from Chicago ON TIME.

If you are meeting someone on that flight, it is reassuring to know that your time in this space will not be long and that your trip has not been wasted. If you are departing with those words, it is good to know that mechanical or weather difficulties are not delaying your trip.

Signboards provide simple information that gives direction for the journey. Consider other signboards in your life. Do you read the Bible? Do you meditate? Do you worship? Where can you hear God's call and find direction?

Signboards are all around. Watch for your arrivals and departures.

Dear Lord, sensitize me to the
signboards of my life.

Being "Bumped"

Airports are often so full of passengers that those waiting at terminals are offered the opportunity to take later flights in return for a free flight at a later date.

I have never been "bumped" from a flight in this manner, but I have friends who have. And I have often been envious of them for managing to win these "free" tickets. Because of luck and their willingness to wait, they could fly wherever they wanted.

This willingness to give up a seat is an interesting action. In a way it is selfless, but in another way, the people who are "bumped" know they will be rewarded. Airlines reward their "selfless" behavior with seats on future flights. I wonder what would happen if there were no incentives provided for "bumped" passengers. Who would give up a perfectly good seat so that another person could travel?

In the flight of life, that is exactly what Jesus did. And amazingly God rewarded Jesus' selfless behavior with our salvation. In a very large sense, you might say that Jesus was "bumped" for our redemption. It is almost too much to comprehend.

Dear Lord, thank you for allowing yourself
to be "bumped" on my behalf.

Eight Hours for a Two Hour Flight

Sometimes there is just no easy way to get there. You live forty- five minutes from the airport. They ask you to check in at least an hour early. Your flight is only an hour long, but it is running thirty minutes late.

Finally you board the plane, but you sit on the runway in an over-heated plane for another thirty minutes before you take off. And once you are in the air, you realize that if you had only begun driving when you left for the airport, you would have been there by now.

You also would not have to contend with baggage check, the rental car company, and the forty-minute drive to your destination at the other end of the flight.

Considering that one of the goals of flying is to make life easier, it is ironic that modern flight is such a major ingredient in the complicated existence many people face daily.

Even in the best of circumstances the time spent in the one-hour flight in my example would have lasted nearly three hours. Unfortunately, as anyone who waits in airports knows, the best of circumstances do not always exist.

Nor do the best of circumstances always exist in life either. Difficult times try our souls. In the end these difficult moments make us stronger people. Still, no one chooses the detours of life when the straight routes are perfectly adequate.

Like the time-consuming flight, the difficult path in life gives us something to talk about later. Hopefully it gives us something to pray about as well. St. Paul said that "all things work together for those who love God." When I hear that passage, I often wonder if St. Paul could have known that one day people would be delayed so often in airline travel.

Lord, help me overcome the delays and rough places of my life.

Airport under Construction

One of the most annoying signs facing anxious travelers on their way to the airport is the sign often seen at the turnoff leading to the parking deck: "Airport under Construction."

Traffic has increased so dramatically at some airports that this sign is visible nearly all the time. The presence of construction creates a dilemma for airport administrators: How do you go about your routine when so many people are taking so long to reach the gates?

The answer is that you don't. If you are an airport administrator, what you do is inform the public to arrive even earlier for their flights because just parking in the airport can be a major hassle.

I doubt heaven will have any construction zones. Even if the place is burgeoning with people, God will accommodate us easily and effortlessly. Heaven is, after all, a perfect place.

If the airport is like the rest of my life, I realize that I am much like the sign. I am "under construction" too. God is still working with me and hopefully I will be better next year than I am today. In the meantime, I suppose that we can hope the same for airports under construction too.

Lord, help me remember that you
are not finished with me yet.

Sliding Doors

As you walk through the automatic doors of the airport, you leave behind one world only to enter another world that is busier and more frenetic. One of the things that strikes me every time I enter a terminal is how hard everyone inside is working. Something always seems to be happening, and the doors are a dividing point between these two worlds.

When you think about life, there are all kinds of doors that distinguish one life from another. Every couple that marries walks hand-in-hand out of doors different than they were as they entered those same doors nervously awaiting the moment of their marriage. They may be the same people, but their lives are forever changed.

Sometimes terminal doors bring about similar changes for the people who enter them. A long-lost relative appears for the very first time. A baby arrives from Russia to meet a new adoptive family. A soldier returns home from basic training. The doors open and close countless times each day. One life ends. Another begins.

Transitions are the fabric of life, and God is in each one of them.

Lord, help me appreciate the changes in my life.

The Air Fortress

A few of them remain. I call them "air fortresses." As you drive up to the airport, you see a rising tower of glass poking its way into the sky. Back in the days when they were new, controllers could have good visibility of the runways from these vantage points.

When I was in kindergarten, we took a tour of our local airport and ascended to the room where the controllers sat. In those days, it felt as if whoever worked in these places possessed an awesome and indescribable power.

Now the old "air fortress" buildings seem a little anachronistic. When you see them in an airport, you wonder why the airport is so small or why the airport authority in the town has not replaced the tower long ago.

Still, there is something reassuring about these places. In many communities airports contain the largest amounts of public land. When a revolution occurs in another country, you always hear about people taking over the airport. And, even in the most modern airports, it feels as if you are entering a kind of fortress as you drive in.

One of the great hymns of the Christian church is "A Mighty Fortress." The hymn reminds us that God alone is the fortress of our lives. As much power as an airport conjures up, it cannot come close to the kind of power that God wields. Airports are simply a reflection of earthly power. Heavenly power is something entirely different.

Lord, help me appreciate the heavenly power you have over my life.

Airlines

As you drive into a large airport for the first time, you need to drive slowly enough to read the signs. Long lists of airlines dot the landscape, and if you drive too fast, you may end up at the wrong terminal.

As I have read these signs over the years, the names of the airlines keep changing. One airline is taken over by another. Another airline goes bankrupt. Still another maintains a more prominent position of the sign because it has acquired more airport gates.

Following the directions on the sign is the first step of faith. While knowing the name of an airline is important to lead you to your point of departure, what is really important is the trust you place in the people behind this name. In order for the system to work, you must trust that the airline you fly on a particular day will bring you safely to your destination in the shortest amount of time possible.

If airlines remembered the act of faith required to fly them, then perhaps some of them would improve their service. Fortunately God is more dependable than the airlines. And, no matter how many things change in the world, God's name remains the same.

Lord, help me sustain the faith I have in you.

The Smithsonian

An entire building at the Smithsonian Institute is devoted to flying. In some ways the story of flying is the story of the twentieth century. So many things have happened and so many improvements have been made that it is easy to forget that people have not yet been flying for an entire century, and they have been flying as passengers on scheduled airlines much less time than that.

Sometimes it is important to reflect on the events that have brought us to where we are now. The plane that you fly today could not take off without the thousands of small innovations that make it possible.

In some ways that is how God works with our lives too. The faith that we know today could never have come to us without the saints who shared it in the past and without the care and devotion of many other ordinary people in our past.

Museums help us appreciate the past and understand the gift that those of the past offer to us in the present.

Lord, thank you for your gifts in my life.

Diversity

When you see the convergence of people walking through the concourse, one of the first things you notice is how different everyone seems. People dress differently. Their skin is different. If you listen, you will hear them speaking different languages. Even if you can only listen for English, you hear dialects.

Many people today feel threatened by the diversity they see around them. They assume that the different ideas or cultures to which they are exposed are a harmful or negative force that must somehow be stopped. On the other hand, many other people sense that diversity is a great gift that must be both tolerated and appreciated.

As you look around the concourse, notice the faces of all of the different people around you. All of these people have the same aspirations and dreams for their children that you do for yours. All of them, like you, are children of God in that God created them all.

When I consider life in that way, it is difficult for me to maintain my prejudices. I begin to ask what different people may have to offer and how faith can be shared with and among them. I begin to see them not from a distance but through the lens of a new and powerful relationship originally cast by God. And before I know it, the world is no longer large. It is simply a family sitting down together at a common table called life.

Lord, help me appreciate the diverse gifts
of people in my life.

Metal Detectors

When you walk into the concourse, one of the first things that you come to are those pesky metal detectors. If you beep as you pass through, the attendant will search you with a smaller device that makes you feel like a criminal.

Most people pass through without being too annoyed by this inconvenient technological innovation. Whenever I pass through one of these devises, I try to forget about how much it is invading my privacy.

God is also like that metal detector. Without my knowing or realizing it, God can peer into my soul. When things are out of balance in my life, it feels as if God knows exactly what I need to set things right. Isn't that really the purpose of prayer? When things are all right, I pass each day as if I were passing through the sensors without a squeak. Things feel right.

Dear Lord, help me appreciate your
knowledge of my life.

AIR TRAVEL
WITH
A PURPOSE

A Loved One Dies

You don't know what to say. You'd rather not be making the flight, but you have to. As you look around, it feels as if you are in a world by yourself.

No one around you seems at all aware of your pain. And when you arrive, you know that the time you spend will be anything but peaceful.

Yet in the midst of the pain is blessing. You would not be going if you did not feel the bond of love pulling on your heart. Maybe you can't quite explain the love, but still it is there. But it is difficult to describe.

As you travel pray for strength and hope—strength to make it through the days ahead of you. Hope in God's everlasting glory and life.

Grieving is never easy. Relationships are difficult to give up. Still there is joy in knowing the peace that God provides in the midst of grief. There is joy in knowing a loved one lives eternally in that peace.

Lord, help me know your peace and help me
reflect that peace with those whom I love.

The Job Offer

When the recruiter called, he said you would talk to these people. The trouble is they are a thousand miles away. Changing jobs means changing your life. New opportunity means new responsibilities.

They say they are paying $10,000 more than you make right now, but is the move really worth it?

As you make this trip questions have been pounding in your head. Some of them are questions of doubt. What if I am not good enough? What if I don't measure up? Can my ego get by if I don't get the offer?

Relax. This is your day, but you are not in complete control. God has a hand in this. When you walk through the polished doors leading to your interview, God will be there too. Pray that God will show you the way to go.

And if you do get the offer? Pray that God will direct you to the right course of action as you pursue your new life. Just remember, God will bring newness to your life whether you move or not.

Lord, help me face the transitions of life with courage and trust in you.

Home for the Holidays

It's been a long time since last Christmas. If you close your eyes, you can remember the sounds of a home filled with people telling stories, singing carols, and having a great time. As you look around, there is a plane full of people fighting the crowds to experience the same things you remember.

Of course there is no guarantee that your experience will be repeated. Maybe going home won't be that easy. Maybe there are one or two fewer people around the table than there were last year.

Holiday memories are great. But holiday times do not always work out as we plan. Reality somehow overcomes expectation. Holiday blues can overwhelm holiday cheer.

Unless of course you remember why you are making the trip in the first place. Holidays have a lot to do with hope. You hope that your life will make a difference. You hope that God has a purpose for you. You hope that human salvation is wrapped up in a tiny child in a manger. And that hope makes all the difference.

There is no way of knowing what you will encounter when you arrive home for the holidays. Only one thing is certain—God's hope is alive in you and you can share that hope with others. That is what joy really means at this time of year.

Lord, help me share your holiday with others and help me know your true joy in my life.

Off to College

Most of your friends have so much to take with them that they are driving to college. Unfortunately the college you chose is on the other side of the country, and you can only take so much with you. You have packed as much as you can, but you have left much behind.

As you sit alone in your seat, you begin to think of all of those things you left behind. You also wonder what kind of life you will discover in this new place. Will it be exciting? challenging? difficult? fun?

No one can know the answers to future life. Major changes often come in moments. No doubt you will see many changes in the days and weeks ahead. And by Christmas break, you will be an entirely different person than you are at this moment.

All you need to remember is that God is at work in whatever you become. Enjoy your life but never forget God's power in the changes that take place.

Lord, help me remember that wherever I go,
there you are.

You Serve

As a flight attendant you have traveled the route many times. You can predict the exact moment that the plane will begin its descent for landing. You know when to take up the trays and when to put them out. You have poured so many drinks that you can taste them on your fingers long after the flight is over. And, you have dealt with more than your share of unruly passengers.

In spite of all of this, there is still something unique about each flight. Never do the people you serve look the same. As you stand and deliver the routine speech about the aircraft safety features, you wonder why you continue to speak because no one seems to be listening.

Then it happens. A passenger smiles and engages you in brief conversation. Serving begins to feel like a real experience. People seem to appreciate the small courtesies you bring to the job. And each time that happens, you feel a small energy at work within you.

Serving on an airplane is not much different from other kinds of serving. Like all serving, it is a gift. If you don't believe that, put yourself in the position of a passenger treated rudely by a flight attendant. Serving is living out a way of life that God shows very clearly in the scriptures. Yours is a high calling.

Lord, help me appreciate the gift of serving others even when I begin to feel it is too difficult to continue.

Flying the Plane

Flying the plane is a great responsibility. There are so many checks that must be made. It feels as if you must be in total control because people are depending on you to get them where they need to go safely. And "safely" is definitely the key word.

You could be overwhelmed by the responsibility if you thought about it too much. Fortunately you do not work alone. You have a crew that works with you, and you also know that your life and theirs are in God's care.

As you begin your flight, pray for a safe journey and say a prayer of thanks each time you sit at the controls for the continuing care of a loving God. As the journey continues, remember that your journey and that of your passengers and crew continues because of God's infinite power of grace.

Lord, help me know more fully that you are the pilot of my life.

Traveling for a Living

Were it not for your "day-timer" you would have no idea where you were going because someone at your company books the flights for you. All you know is that for the deal to work, you have to be in Kansas City tomorrow.

Sometimes you wonder whether you are "making a living" or "making a life." Those times when you can remain at home seem more and more precious. You can tell when the travel is becoming too much when you just want to stay home for your vacation.

You often worry about the things you are missing or whether your children will grow up without you. As you look out at the azure sky, you wish you could hear the voices you left behind.

Being a "road warrior" is not an easy life. It is particularly difficult if you fail to make the spiritual connections that keep your life centered in the Lord. Take some time as you travel to find that center. Close your eyes. Relax for a moment. Permit yourself to think of home. And know that you can find a true home in the heart of God.

Lord, help me always to feel your comfort and care.

Solving a Problem

Where you are does not seem to be working. Maybe with a change of scenery, life will look different. You are flying to a place with different scenery.

A fresh start. A new life. A different approach. All of these phrases reflect a spiritual understanding. The word that describes these things is "resurrection."

As you look for a different place, don't just look at the scenery. Look for the sources of resurrection in your life. Which of the new things that you encounter are really life-changing? In which areas do you really need to change your life? Where is the Lord in this picture?

Most of the time when people look for a change of scenery, they forget that the real changes that need to occur are inside themselves. Pray that the Lord will direct the changes taking place as you move to a new place. Pray that you will gain new and vital relationships with others as you embark on your quest.

Dear Lord, help me live each day
as a new adventure you have provided.

Working the Deal

They told you that you had to be in Dallas on Tuesday. The deal would not go through unless you were there to shepherd it along.

The problem is that you told your daughter you would be home in time for her birthday party at 5 p.m. If things go perfectly, you will have just enough time to catch the afternoon flight and still make it for the party.

Life is a tightrope sometimes. Deals are important—relationships are more important. No one wished for more time spent on dealmaking at the close of life. Lots of people have regretted not taking time to cement the close relationships of their lives.

As you travel today, pray for the deal to go through. Birthdays only happen once a year.

Dear Lord, help me pay attention to the really important parts of my life.

Friends

It's been two years since you last saw your college roommate. You know that when you arrive, you will pick up where you left off. You can hardly bear the excitement of seeing your friend again.

Still, there is a little uncertainty. Things have changed since the last time you were together. You have taken on different relationships. You aren't sure whether or not you will still have anything in common. All you can do is remember the good times you spent together.

It's important to know that friendship is an enduring gift from God. The things that shaped you as you grew together in friendship will still shape you now. Don't worry. God's Spirit continues to direct this relationship and all relationships you experience. Just be open to that Spirit, and it will never let you down.

Thank you, God, for all of my friendships and for your Spirit at work in my life.

Lovers

As you sit on the plane or in the concourse, your whole body begins to ache with the sort of gnawing feeling you experienced the last time you were apart and about to get back together. It's funny that the feeling is so difficult to describe, and you are glad that it doesn't come along too often.

"Flight 2106 is now boarding." The words seem so insignificant as they float into the open air. Yet, for you, those words mean that you are a little bit closer to seeing the person who is waiting for you at the other end of the flight.

You remember the look on this person's face the last time you were together. And you remember the way your eyes touched each other as you entered a hug for a final embrace. Loving is such a great feeling. If you could only keep the feeling you had as you were hugging forever.

On the other hand, if you felt it all the time, how would you know the gnawing feeling you have now as you think of your lover was such a special feeling?

Lord, help me relish my special feelings
and thank you for the gift of intimacy
you have brought to my life.

Meeting a Parent

Looking across the aisle in the waiting room, you spot a child being escorted to a seat by a flight attendant. A mother reaches down and hugs the child, as she provides specific instructions on what will happen when the father meets her in the airport at the end of the flight.

Life is full of complications and disruptions. The little girl didn't have anything to do with her family falling apart or with the fact that her father had to take a job so far away. She just wants to see her daddy again.

Distance and time are the great dividing points in our lives. In the Middle Ages (aside from the fact there were no airplanes), this scene would have been unthinkable. People lived and died in the same places. Now if something happens 5,000 miles away, we know about it in an instant, and if we need to be there, we can make it in a few hours.

Knowing how much the world has changed probably won't provide much comfort for the child traveling alone. When you think about it, she is a picture of everyone else on the plane. In life we travel alone with the simple faith that a loving father is waiting for us on the other side.

Lord, help me find hope when time and distance separate me from those I love.

Recreation

It's great when you can fly just for the fun of it. You've been working without a break for a long time, and you feel the need for recreation.

When you hear the word "recreation," you don't usually associate it with what it means when you break it apart. To be re-created sounds odd. Why would you want to be re-created? What you have isn't good enough?

Some people might answer that what they have is never good enough. They need to re-create themselves all the time.

Recreation is really a spiritual opportunity. You can take time off, go to a different place, and come back refreshed and invigorated. When your recreation happens that way, it truly is a gift from God. You might just think you have been on a really good vacation, but God has been working with you all along. God has enabled you to be re-created. Maybe that is what all journeys in life are about.

Dear Lord, help me appreciate your care in the fun times as well as the serious times of my life.

Because You're the Parent

One of the airlines ran an advertisement that included a scene in which a father walked in on his daughter's dance recital. The story was that he had flown a certain airline and had succeeded in arriving on time for the recital after a busy day in another city.

I thought the advertisement was really a dramatization of conflicting responsibilities. On the one hand was the responsibility of the job, and on the other was the genuine responsibility of attending a child's dance recital.

Most people don't have much trouble choosing between their children and work. Very few people for instance say that they would have liked to have attended more business meetings as they look back at their lives.

The problem is that the tensions in our lives force us to make choices we would rather not make. The advertisement seemed to indicate that the man really could find a way to be in two places. Sometimes however, that does not happen. Sometimes job responsibilities outweigh responsibilities to a family. Sometimes relationships suffer as people make these difficult choices.

If you are rushing home in order to be with your child, take time to give thanks for the one whom you are rushing to see. And thank God for helping you make the difficult choices every day.

Lord, keep me safe and help me appreciate all of your gifts in my life.

133

You Really Didn't Mean to Go Through Atlanta

People used to say that whether you go to heaven or hell, you would have to change planes in Atlanta. Like other hub cities, Atlanta has the distinction of being visited by many people who have no interest in being there.

The problem is that in order for you to arrive at your destination, sometimes there are side trips that take you to a different place. In life these side trips might be summarized by the word "serendipity."

Serendipity happens all the time. Some people say that serendipity is actually providence. Things happen because God means for them to happen, but there are really no coincidences in life.

You may not have meant to go to Atlanta, but something could happen there that could change your life. St. Paul didn't really know when he went to Damascus that he would meet Jesus on the road, but when he did, the world was changed. St. Patrick didn't think that being kidnapped to Ireland was a good thing, but had it not happened the Irish people would not have known the Lord.

You can probably think of many instances when things happened in your life that took you on a detour and changed your life.

So if you really didn't mean to go through Atlanta, take heart. There will be many places that you don't mean to go on the journey of life but some of those places will turn out to be gold mines.

Lord, help me appreciate the
random times of my life.

Socked In

Sometimes fog is so dense in one airport that planes must land somewhere else. When this happens, it feels as if your destination no longer exists. There is no way to arrive easily, and no one knows exactly how long the fog will last.

There are times when life feels this way too. You are looking forward to accomplishing a goal, and you wonder if you can make it. Suddenly it feels as if you are "socked in." No matter where you turn, you cannot see clearly the path you should take. You feel confused, lost, and alone. And, you wonder what consequences will come to you as a result of your inability to act.

Turning to God in prayer is a good way to lift the fog that you encounter in life. After you have placed your decision in God's hands, it always seems clearer and more intelligible.

One of the expressions that people use to describe this situation is: "Things are always darkest just before dawn." I wonder if whoever said that first assumed that things would be darkest because people try so hard to depend on themselves that they cannot see God's light beyond the turmoil of this life.

When the fog burns away, the morning is usually bright and serene as the sun bathes the landscape and brilliant color replaces the dullness of a previously gray day. May this happen in your life before your flight reaches its conclusion.

Lord, help me see through the fog in this world and know your true and brilliant light.

Witness Protection

You are not sure exactly where you are going because you are part of a "witness protection program." To be sure, this is not very likely but you may have made wrong choices in your life that have led you into a place you did not really want to go.

You may as well be in some kind of program because it feels as if you are getting in over your head. The problem is that when you land you don't know exactly what you will do or how you can discover a new life.

If you are reading these words, you can begin a new life. All you have to do is place the overwhelming troubles and concerns that weigh you down into God's hands. Jesus promises in the scriptures that "his yoke is easy and his burden is light." If you place your burden on his shoulders, then it will always be easier to bear.

You may not believe that it works, but it does. Take a deep breath, close your eyes, and speak these words over and over in your mind: "Lord, I am yours and you are mine. New life is what I pray to find." Many others have found that life, and so can you.

Lord, help me find a new life.

"Star Trek"

Except for the fact that you are flying far above the ground, it probably does not feel like you are traveling between the planets. When you decided to fly, you probably did not identify yourself as a "trekkie."

Nevertheless, one of the reasons that the "Star Trek" reality has been around for more than a generation is that the premise of intergalactic travel causes so much curiosity. You don't really need to travel to other planets in the universe. You can just think about it.

Life is full of destinations that seem profound and vague. There are all kinds of places that you can go in your mind that are beyond your physical limitations. Journeys of the mind are one of the great gifts of existence. If you could not venture beyond the limitations of your life, you could not enjoy all kinds of things you take for granted.

When you think about it long enough, you realize that "Star Trek" is much more real than you originally thought. You really cannot know the destination of your life. You really cannot know the places and events that God has placed before you. All you can know is where you are going right now.

As you consider the various places that you might go, pray for the vision and the wisdom to appreciate your destinations in life. And, wherever your journey takes you, may you live long and prosper.

Lord, only you provide the destinations of my life.
Give me the assurance to know
that you are with me wherever I go.

Jetfuel

Although you might not consider this fact while the plane is racing down the runway at the beginning of your flight, an aircraft uses a huge portion of its fuel supply on take-off. It stands to reason. The force required for the plane to become airborne is enormous. And, as the engines rev up to an unbearable roar during those first seconds, they are concentrating that force for the flight ahead.

There are many examples of this concentration of force in other experiences: A car uses less fuel cruising down the highway than when it is going up a hill. A fighter concentrates energy in training long before the fight begins. A politician struggles each day talking to many individuals before significant poll numbers appear in news reports.

If you consider your most successful undertaking in life, you probably realize that success meant that you concentrated your efforts for a period of time. You succeeded in this endeavor because you were able to focus intensity and effort into the undertaking. Chances are you were not successful simply because you were lucky. You had to work hard in order to gain the result.

In a sense, perseverance, hard work and determinations are the "jetfuels" of life. Without these attributes, we could not accomplish very many things. Sometimes, after we have exerted much effort toward a goal, we can coast along and enjoy the benefits of our efforts. At the same time, if we rest for too long, we may also see the things for which we worked fall apart. Many people have experienced the pain and disappointment that came from losing focus and drive in life.

Just as an airplane expends fuel at different rates during a flight, people expend varying amounts of effort in the things they do. However, if you want to succeed in life, you have to know what the engines are telling you: If you focus on a goal and pursue it with diligence and perseverance, God will direct you toward a successful life.

God, give me the strength to persevere.

ABOUT THE AUTHOR

Mark Scott presently serves as pastor of Shades Valley Evangelical Lutheran Church in Birmingham, Alabama. He has also served congregations in Atlanta, Georgia and Knoxville, Tennessee. He holds a Doctor of Ministry degree from Emory University, and is Chairman of the Board of Trustees for Newberry College.

When he is not traveling, Dr. Scott enjoys family life at home with his wife Karen and their three daughters while working on his next book.

ORDER FORM

Please send _____copies of FLIGHTS OF FAITH at
$10.95 per copy. (Postage for one book is $2.00, add $1.25
for each additional copy in the same shipment. Alabmaa
residents add 4% sales tax.)

Name _____

Address _____

City _____ State_____ Zip_____

Send check or Money Order to:

> Magnolia Mansions Press
>
> 4661 Pinewood Drive
>
> Mobile, AL 36618
>
> Email: magnoliamansions@aol.com

Charge to:

MasterCard or VISA card Number:_____

Expiration Date: ____/ ____/ _____

Signature of Cardholder: _____

Name and address of cardholder if different from above:

Name _____

Address _____

City _____ State_____ Zip_____